Unstoppal

GW00390988

The Basics of Growing And The Anatomy Of Happiness

By

MONICA PERIADE

Terms and Conditions

LEGAL NOTICE

Published by Babysteps Publishing Limited All enquires to kevin@babystepspublishing.com

ISBN-13 9798783571282

Table of Contents

Dedication

This book is dedicated to the " Unstoppable You " my reader, my critic, my hero, as well to my Godson and Goddaughter David and Davina, to Sofia and Nicolas and all the children in the whole wide world. I only hope it will inspire and give you the extra wind you need to reinforce your wings and never have to doubt yourself.

And finally, to everyone that has been there for me. You know who you are.

With much love Monica

Introduction

When God made man, he gave him his absolute wisdom! Which Is in you!

Success is not something that just happens overnight, although it feels that way looking from the outside; I assure you that for so many of us, it's a really long journey of hard work and persuasion.

All successes start with ONE, one thought, one step, one action followed by another, one restriction after another, one idea, one decision, one sale, one order, one client, one day after many.

Accomplishing anything "great" in your life requires time, effort, focus, energy, desire, creativity, and while I am certain you already know this, remember that this is a great reminder.

Everything takes time: birth and breeding takes time, blooming takes time, the foundation takes time, building takes time, a society, a generation, a relationship, building trust takes time, and so does it's growing.

Every season has its own time, sunset and sunrise have their own time, so you will. So have patience and trust the process, trust yourself, search and believe you will find your own way in your own time. Give yourself the time you need to become what you need to become in order for you to be as you may: a phoenix, a lion, a breeze, successful, happy, or all.

When you are not used to being confident, being confident feels like arrogance.

When you are not used to meeting your own needs prioritizing yourself feels like selfishness.
When you are not used to asking for help doing so makes you feel needy.

When you are not happy, settling for less feels normal.
When you are in a passive state for a very long time, becoming assertive feels aggressive.
When you are not familiar with love being used and control fees like love

Sometimes we can't see things as they are because we are too used to something that we shouldn't be in the first place.
Healing and growing start with the need to do so and the decision to change your life around. You can make the necessary changes alone or seek professional help to smooth and speed the process.

Time, the most important element, is having the time or giving the time to find what you really want, your drive, and once you discover and decide what that is, then dedicate your full time and energy to (your personal dream).

So it is not about having the time. It's about making time. How many times have we said: If only I had the time for this or when you actually have the time, but this invaluable resource needs to be managed fully.

Don't ever compare yourself; if you are ahead, it's just a matter of time until someone else will be ahead of you, and if you are behind, it's simply again a matter of time until you will get ahead in life.

Effort, the conscious effort, is an essential element that will pay off eventually, no matter what. And is the main attributor that will influence all the other factors that will get you to success. It's not about being strong; it is about putting in the effort.

What is effort, if not the ability to put all your energy into something that you really want for yourself?

Time & Efforts: You can achieve almost anything if you put in enough time and effort.

3

Focus is a must-do at times to keep you going and get you to produce the material, steps, and support you need in your journey. Focus intentionally, laser focus, as I like to call it. What you focus on expands; if you focus on the love, you manifest more love in your life, if you focus on the money, you will find ways to make money, I am not here to judge how, if you focus on good things more good things in your life will manifest itself. If you focus on giving, more will come into your life that you will be able to keep on giving. If your focus is your image, then you will create the exact image you want for yourself. Focus is finding; the focus is manifesting.

Your focus and energy go where you will find the time, the discipline, and drive for it.

Drive is a constant feeling that you have to have, and eventually, it will pay off with creativity. It's your personal ability to stay motivated even when no signs of assurance or confirmation of what you work to accomplish.

Curiosity is as curious as a child; it is pivotal to be curious, absorb, and have that curiosity for things in line with your needs, wants, desires, and goals.

Goals: Start with writing down your goals and then the skills you need to achieve those goals and the exact step. Goals and planning are essential in your path to success. You already know all that; all you need is to take real action. Tony Robbins said: *It's not* *about the goal; it's about growing to become the person that can accomplish that goal.* Do you see? It will help if you become a goal setter, a planner, a follow-through, a laser focus, a skilled, driven master.

If you want to become a famous dancer, you have to develop a dancer's skills and then take those skills to the level of an outstanding dancer. Goals are a never-ending list in someone's life, and they are one of the healthiest to-do lists.

You have health, relationship, wealth, career, love, and passion when it comes to goals and achievements.

You have twelve months in the calendar, write down as many goals as you want, divide them between these twelve months, and then laser focus on each one. Before you do that, prioritize that list of goals.

Understanding yourself is pivotal, and I mean really understand who you are and decide who you should be and be as thoughtful and considerate as possible in the process of becoming who you are meant to be and that your inner self craves for you to be.

Being a wife is wonderful. But maybe you also want to be a wonderful ballerina, a poet, a jogger, a surfer, a bohemian, the reliable wise person to your inner circle.

And while you didn't pursue that early in life, trying to understand, what other than a ballerina you wish to be, is a milestone to personal growth.

Being a self-sufficient single-man engineer might be enough for a while, but at some point, in time, you will find yourself craving for something else, more than just that, and this is what I meant when I said understand yourself and listen to your little inner voice in the background.
Who do you want to be, and who do you need to be to reach your final truth.

Once we understand how we have become the person we are today and why we are conforming or settling to whatever life we settle, we can only plan a lasting empowering change.

We can take back the power of our minds and decisions only by understanding why we do what we do, why we are the type of person we are, and why we like or dislike certain things or certain people.

Why you do what you do every day is where you will find empowerment or disempowerment.

Why I Wrote This Book?

I always dreamt of writing a book for the same reason inventors, the magicians of evolution, offer the world their great inventions to enhance the quality of people's lives.

When I first started to write this book, it happened after years and years of procrastination, negative self-talk, and plenty of years of self-sabotaging every bit of a chance I would have to better myself.

I wrote this book to express my love for the world and humankind, especially those of you who, just like me, wish to improve their lives, grow stronger, and help the people they care about.

Another simple reason is explained in simple words: "*Verba volant, Scripta manent,*" which translated means: "spoken words fly away, written words remain."

I hope, and maybe at the risk of coming across as self-important, I know that you will become a weapon for your growth as you finish reading this book. I compressed decades of thoughts and wisdom into days and nights of writing this book for you to like and use.

Please do, if you can simply carry it with you or have it within easy reach so when you get into the need for a boost, remember me, I've been there right where you are, and it wasn't so bad apart from one big reason only: it got me where I am today.

I often wonder *"why me"* the trap we all so often fall into the first time we hit the ground. I often wondered if I was making the right choices or heading in the right direction, and in past years the major question was If I was ever going to make it or I would simply torment myself into the **neverhappeningland**.

I want to thank my family and many "friends" for all the pain and wounds they caused me.

I want to thank every human being who has rejected, used, or humiliated me because I wouldn't have become so humbled.

I wouldn't understand what powerful force love is, and how healing a smile can be, or the lacking, the rejection, the importance of self-acceptance, the means of getting a chance, the value of a hand in need, and all of that if I never went through all the drama of these terrible experiences.

Please trust yourself, the value of your own existence, and if you feel that you're unimportant, well…you couldn't be more wrong.

Why Should You Read This Book?

What this book will do for you?

This book will elevate your thinking and will probably give you that motivation, the resources to go on, or the material to find your path.

Being strong and resourceful is the only way and writing this book is a gift to people in need for a ray of hope and to all the readers to see that pain leads you to gain. There is a meaning for everything that happens to us, that we can use our imagination and the results of our mind in our favor as simply as everything we want is within reach.

It's a book meant to encourage, motivate, and influence in the simplest and the best possible way, inspired from my life experiences, the pieces of knowledge I acquired while I was struggling, from the ability to listen to my own instincts and that beautiful, positive, vibrant inner voice.

It's a book about how not to give up, effortlessly work on yourself, and how focusing on helping others eventually turns back to us in beautiful ways. It is about as much as tears, as much as love, joy, and prosperity.

I hope my wonderful reader will turn into that strong force and will take full charge of their life, of how they want to live, and how much joy they should keep in their hearts.

It is from me and the universe to you, my beautiful human; please take advantage and change your life into a world of fulfillment.

I promise if you read this book to the end, you will be entertained, feel understood, shocked, and closer to me and life's predictabilities.

The surest way to interfere with your growth is by saying: oh, but I know all that....and it didn't make a 'dime' for me.

Chapter 1

Introduction to Yourself

The story we tell ourselves silently in our minds is what creates our everyday reality. Monica Periade

The power of understanding, change, and adapting.

Remember the famous Henry Ford quote, *"Whether you think you can, or you think you can't – you're right,"* and that emphasizes how much attitude determines success or failure.

Repeat to yourself: I can, and I will, End of Story! No doubts whatsoever.

"At the center of your being, you have the answer; you know who you are, and you know what you want." Lao Tzu

You're bigger than your imagination and grander than the length of your life, you can achieve the unimaginable, and you can destine to last forever.

Under all that we are, there is all we can be, and it only takes as little as an inner conversation.

Introspection is a powerful tool and art itself. Being introspective, understanding, and personal intuitivism is the path to endless possibilities.

It is one thing to understand what you have been taught. It is another to understand things through your experiences and through your unique perception this time, to understand, empathize, consider, and select all through your own filter.

Knowledge, information all become powerful if we realize how to use everything in favor and make things to serve us.
What we believe is either a way of limiting ourselves or a way to grow stronger and better for what is suitable and best for you.

Your level of perception and understanding will propel, highjack your ticket to success and sustain all your desires. So, you see here "why" understanding is an art?

We all have the same nervous system, neurons, organs, etc.; for some, these are stronger(fiercer) because they use the power of (understanding). Therefore, if we only give attention and understanding to our personal reasonings, we are definitely limiting ourselves.

What we believe is either a way of limiting ourselves or a way to grow stronger and better.

When you change the way you look at things, you change the meaning of those things; when you change the meanings, then you directly change your life. So when you change your level of understanding (your perceptions), you are starting to master your life, which is not something you hear of for the first time.

What better progress can you make than changing in a world where the only constant we have is "Change". Change the way you expect things from others; when you change that, your expectations for appreciation are changing, and your life becomes abundantly enriched.

The question is, how to change the way we look at things?!

Well, as I study my own improvements and the results of remarkable people, from my personal experiences, I can confidently tell you that by unlearning most of the things and thoughts that have been enforced on us under the term of education or various other forms.

Although, please don't get me wrong, mostly we have been thought out of great intentions, so we are not here to dismiss what we've been taught but to unlearn so we can learn only what is relevant to our own path.

Change is a phenomenon, a constant in our lives, a tool, and by understanding change, you can master your life. If you assume that things will always be the way they are in your life, you couldn't be more wrong, and if you assume that this is how you are and you will always be, then think again.

Life changes every single moment, and so do you. You cannot change your life as you need to evolve unless you're changing how you think, perceive, and behave; if you always do what you always did, you will always get what you always got.

I remember days when I confused the meaning of change, consistency and adapting to changes and how hard I was on myself. All that conflict was influenced by everything that I was taught or heard around me with no clue who I was, wanted to be, or what I wanted to become.

In fact, I have discovered the love for my daily long walks as an alternative to my unending questions of why I am here, what my purpose is, and what life is, and because I was in the middle of the noise, I couldn't hear or see the path.

I didn't have it all placed together and within reach as I grew up, but I did search for meaning and purpose; I wanted to bring value, contribute, and understand the "being" from the first day I could remember.

I could understand much, but I had questions, and what my reader here wants to take out that understanding starts with questioning.

What's one of the worst mistakes you can ever make in your journey to success? Surprisingly enough, it is being satisfied with where you are and even taking what you have for granted. I don't mean you have to stress yourself or avoid enjoying what you have accomplished but getting comfortable with where you are even if it's not as far as you want it to be, or maybe you look back and say I have come a long way and this is how far I can go.

It's also drifting through life, waiting to see where the current will take you instead of forging your own path.
The results you have or don't have, the life you lead now, are based on the decision you made, and you manage to grow because at times, were not satisfied with what you had or where you were and wanted more for yourself.

Dream. I know it sounds idealistic and not like something you don't know already, but although it is something we do throughout our entire life and since we were born, so many of us refrain from dreaming.

We know, many people out there stay in unsatisfying jobs, a career that is not in line with their passions, low-paid jobs, toxic environments, and sometimes on bare necessities, making a living or even making plenty of money but without a purpose or a dream.

I know it because I used to be one of those people for a good portion of my life. But, unfortunately, by not dreaming and simply reasoning my doings, I wasted a good part of my life that I could have used in more value.

I lost both my parents while I was still very young, which introduced me to life's uncertainties, and the feeling itself amplified the emotion that made me think that life is very uncertain, and while it is, this is not the way anyone should live.

Visions. Visions are the unachievable dreams that turn into reality, and they are essential parts of the human experience; if you have them, you are supposed to pursue them to reach fulfillment. However, if you limit yourself and consider your dream just a simple intangible goal, you may also want to understand what you lose in doing so. Therefore, always understand the consequences of your ''*doing*'' but more, much more importantly, the consequences of your' ''*not doing*''.

Dreams are in your mind for a reason, and only once you start to envision them do they start to come to life; they become tangible as everything that begins in your mind becomes real once we imagine it vividly and repeatedly.

Imagining your dreams with passion will fill your brain and body with pure joy and energy, and that is not something you can afford or should miss out on.

Whatever your dreams are, they are there in your mind for a reason. They could be anything, such as moving mountains, changing countries, owning a business, an island or a building, having your own family, children, all that while the odds are against, creating an app, a video game, publishing a book, becoming an astronaut. . . etc.
And by pursuing your dreams and against all odds, you will have the greatest experiences possible on the way to making them real.

But what if I fail, one often asks?

It is not precisely about getting them but about the experience of pursuing them, which is about what and who you become in the process. It will help if you become the receiver of your dream as you are making your dream come true.
Your dreams are about what you become and what you experience and create while chasing your dream. Envision!

Failure?

You never fail, you only learn new ways or new things you should avoid, but you never actually fail; even the word exists and is often used; YOU simply never FAIL, you become wiser, better equipped, closer to your ultimate goal.

What you do after you fail to achieve that score, that result is what matters the most. Failure should influence your next step positively, and for that, your thinking, mindset, thoughts are to be set on a positive mode.

Every failure brings with the seed of an equivalent or greater success. Practical dreamers don't quit. Napoleon Hill
Desire is key, and failure should not kill your desire, your zest for life and success.

There are no secrets to success. It is the result of preparation, hard work, and learning from failure. –Colin Powell-

Thoughts?

We are the only creatures that have thoughts about having thoughts, and this is called having a conscious mind…which we can use in our pursuit of happiness, joy, and success.

Your conscious mind conducts your life, and your subconscious mind conducts your conscious mind.
The Conscious and The Subconscious mind are always connected; the trick here is to be aware of both.

When we learn to manage our minds, then anything is possible. Absolutely anything, and we see it often in some people's lives, and we wonder how they made it.

An important key in mastering your own mind is understanding how the mind works.

The mind has three basic functions: "**THINK**", followed by "**FEEL**", "**DESIRE**".

These three functions are influenced by our native tendencies to put ourselves first, the influences of our immediate environment, and the capacity to rationalize things. In other words, the way we understand or see things by our first base nature.

These three functions are also majorly influenced by one's egocentrism that is biological-driven. Understanding how exactly your mind works and developing the skills to become a master of your mind. Understanding the mind, how it functions with the psychological tendency towards egocentrism, and the capacity to rationalize.

Everyone thinks that's a fact. It's in our nature as we are equipped to think, is the main function of the mind that is followed by the feeling and desire, but our thinking is determined and altered by various factors: surrounding, environment, and OUR OWN thinking (the self). Our mind also feels and wants, and our thinking determines our thought, and our thoughts determine the others two functions: feeling and desire.

Once you take the time to understand the process of the mind and its basic function, then you can do anything, achieve about anything, including your biggest dream, no matter how big it may seem to you right now.

Feeling and desire to influence our thoughts and that eventually shapes our destiny. How we think and become motivates our choices in life, paths, personal touch, or contribution.

The practice of thinking produces emotions; it also produces desires that influence our thinking once they become too powerful. So, our minds (inner thoughts, feelings, and desires) become a vicious cycle that falls under the direct influence of our native egocentrism or our dominant rationalization.

It's either you are driven by your ego or by reasoning.

In other words, if our native egocentrism directs us, we see the world through a narrowed, selfishly altered perception. We become concerned only with ourselves, our personal needs, and never how our behaviour affects others. We are mostly concerned with what we want and how to validate our wants, beliefs, points, views, desires and never with anything out of our interest.

That affects the people we love, the people who love us, the people we interact with, or the ones that could be a significant part of our success. The key in understanding how the duality of the mind works:

The egocentrism (being trapped in delusions, illusions, and mythises) and reasonably (freeing itself from the first).

Even those three functions of the mind are equally developed, equally essential, and surprisingly equally accessed but not simultaneously; it is only through our thinking that we can finally decide which drives us, control us, and only through our thinking can we master the three functions. I know it might sound complex or complicated, but I promise it is not.
Remember the 'Short Introduction' chapter? Give it some time, effort, and focus, and you will master your life.

Let's go a bit deeper into this process.

BASIC FUNCTIONS OF THE MIND: THINKING ⟹
FEELING ⟹ DESIRE.

The thinking is the part that comprehends life's events, creates and defines problems, situations, initiates or dismisses them. It is the exact function that tells us everything, to notice things, pick up information, and it kind of tells us what is happening to us, but all of that in collaboration with the function of feeling that creates the emotions and that which makes the desire.

So we have two types of emotions, natural and unnatural emotions.

The natural ones are the ones that we all repeatedly experience throughout our life, and the unnatural ones are the ones that are inflicted in full consciousness.
The function of feeling generated by the thinking evaluates the situations we are in as being positive or negative: this feels good, this is great, or this is not really going great for me.

Desires are the ones that give the energy to our actions and define them as possible and desirable: this is valuable, this is worth it, this is good for me, or simply I don't like it, or it's of no use to me.

This means that we can control to our advantage and to others what it's happening to us and what we do.

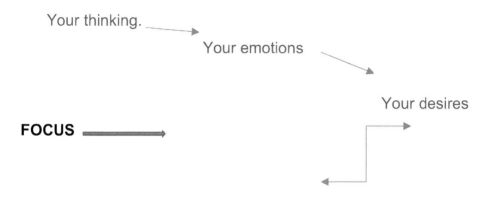

Turn Information into knowledge

Turn knowledge into wisdom

Turn wisdom into choices

Turn Choices into fulfillment

YOUR NOTES

Chapter 2
Your Decisions

Sometimes, we stay in the wrong place, the wrong relationship, job, etc., only because deep down, we believe this is the best we can do. So it's not the fear as much; we think that this is the best we can do.

Your thoughts create and control your feeling and desires, and in fact, those influences your thoughts. Once you understand the vicious cycle and control your thinking, you master your mind and shape your destiny.

Your thoughts are creating your life; your thoughts are pivotal in the quality of your life.

If you think you're a failure, you will feel like a failure; then, you are going to act like a failure and eventually think like a failure—a vicious cycle.

It is where your thoughts are constantly going that you are going to discover all that you need, want, and can. In the inner dialog, you start to shape your destiny in your inner thoughts.

Every single person on this planet earth has the ability to tap into their personal power and create the life that they desire, a life that they enjoy living—a life of meaning, a life with a purpose.

As I repeat myself in this book and in my speeches and workshops, it all starts with a very simple but critical self-question: What do you really, really want? Why do you really, really want that?

Now, do you have a clear vision of what is that you want, desire, crave?

What is that you want in your life and why? In your relationships, your health, love life, business? What is that you want to get from all that? How do you want your life to be, your relationship with others, with your significant other, your relationship with yourself, and your level of health/fitness? How do you want your business to be and why? Now, is it going to make you happy? Write your answer and make even the tiniest decision.

Before you go any further, please don't forget to ask yourself: What do you want to give and why?

I love you, dear reader, and I am certain that you're going to pull through, and you're going to make a success out of the story. It's in you, and you can find it. Bring your own life to live.

Decision

You have the final say, the final vote is yours, as you decide, and no one and nothing else, not your conditions and not your circumstances, will have the final vote in who you become. So, It's your mindset, the decision, and the steps you take that have the ultimate vote in shaping your life, your success, your destiny.

The Power of Making a decision and stepping into that action is not a chapter I would tend to be short on writing. As we grow, we make attempts; we progress; we grow and outgrow things, places, people, and we realize that we make decisions after decisions.

Still, as soon as we need to consciously decide, we freeze completely; we start doubting, worrying, overthinking, and over-analyzing. We even postpone as in forever making that decision.

Sometimes we think we decided, but without an action that comes from that decision, you never have decided but simply engage in thought. It's simply more of an agreement that is not signed, and sealed remains a kind of discussion.

We are not simply coincidences; we are results of our decisions, and sometimes due to lack of planning, the circumstances appear in delays. Our decision and action create possibilities, and the possibility builds us.

I look back into my life and understand that every decision I ever made conditioned my next move and eventually determined where I am today.

Tony Robbins said: *"I believe it is our decisions, not our conditions, that determines our destiny. "* and God knows his words open endless possibilities for many.

I often exemplify: there is no use in being a great swimmer if you live in the middle of the desert, but your decision to change your proximity to a favorable one will determine how accomplished you can be as a swimmer.

The power of creating your own destiny can be achieved by deciding and stepping into action and into totally new energy.

By realizing that at any given time, our life could change to a whole new degree with one decision we took or take, we realize what a powerful tool we have in creating a destiny to our life: DECISION.

To improve our lives, we must direct our lives, and in order to do that, we have to be in consistent control of our actions, of how, when, and how consistent we act. The power of our action consists in the consistency of our actions rather than seldom actions.

Our decisions, good or bad, are determined by our why and how we made them, not necessarily by the consequences, and I will explain in detail why:

We are not always going to make the right decision, and deciding by all the right reasons will influence your state of mind, level of self-trust, and confidence in making future decisions more quickly and far better.

We have to realize that we are not always going to make the right decisions but not deciding at all will allow other people to make the decisions for us, and their decision will have more chances to impact you negatively in the long run more than the one we make for ourselves, as they don't weigh the pros and cons from the same angle as we do.

We have to have a healthy level of self-confidence to make and take decisions as we need.

The Unstoppable You know that avoiding decisions is far worse than making a bad decision, as it allows others to make decisions that will be disagreeable with what we want in the long run.

The reader knows that the only way we can ensure joy and happiness in our life is through the value we put in our decisions and our timing and by aligning them with our personal values.

It's in our personal values and the value of our decision that we create the quality of the life we lead, and even sometimes we fear or doubt, it's always better to learn from failures and mistakes than to have stayed in the same place. What you avoid is usually that one step closer to what you want.

YOUR NOTES

Chapter 3

The Power of Disempowerment

Procrastination and Self Sabotage

Procrastination reflects self-sabotage and is predominantly characteristic of the avoider or the perfectionist. To overcome procrastination, we have to work thoroughly on our level of self-confidence. We mostly procrastinate because we don't believe in that task, think it is hard, or fear failure.

Fear is a man's best enemy; it stops you from achieving and keeps you in a "safe" mode. If we make an effort and put in the time and attention to study what we fear, why we fear, and when we feel frightened the most, we clearly have better chances at overcoming limitations, sabotage, and delays.

Everything that we think and do can work against us or for us, and it all depends on what we decide to do about the things that impact our day-to-day lives and how quick we are in making changes, adapting, and taking charge in our actions.

What is happening to us can simply happen for us. Even that might be something that discourages us, and by that, I mean if you pay attention to your habits, choices, you will discover fears, likes, couldn't and shouldn't, and if you pay attention to the things that didn't go your way you will find a new way and that will usually be the way that is meant for you.

Procrastination isn't a terrible thing as long as you don't let it take too much space in your choices, and it could be a good thing up to a point. Still, however, by definition, procrastination means putting things on hold for far too long, analyzing the cause of it and what it says "about" you and the relation to what you put on hold.

The avoider procrastinator type is the one that is afraid of changes or the one that fears not being able to show up as the world expects it. But, at the same time, the perfectionist has a giant ego and believes more than anything in perfection, showing a deeply hidden fear of not being good enough.

Learning to face right then and there what you need to do and why you won't do it is a hugely important step into your personal success.

Learning to seek to understand why something did not happen the way we planned is a way to find a better way that will serve us to reach where we need.

How often we hear ourselves or others saying: " *if I only had the time,*" and in fact, years later, looking back, all that we had more than anything was time. Did you know that " if I only have the time" originates from a stubborn thought encrypted in our mind and is similar to the causes of procrastination?

What we say to ourselves or others is another way of justifying our own procrastination, our self-sabotage.

Practice: Exercise how you rationalize not doing things, how you justify your behavior in your head, which can be failures, lack of initiative, etc.

Old thoughts are old beliefs, and old beliefs become old habits, and you must have realized by now that old habits die old, which means they first create a lot of chaos in our lives.

Stubbornness – God, I know better

Flexibility is game-changing to your entire world, the way you perceive things, the way you select, make choices, and the way you will plan the course of your life.

One should have the flexibility to change his mind if a better theory, idea, mindset, way, mode, perspective comes his way.

Suppose you have a mind stretched by "unfortunate" experiences, and you understand how positive this is. In that case, you won't limit yourself and develop a very flexible and open mentality that can serve you achieve instead of not. Show up for yourself when you need the most, referring here when you tend to be stubborn and instead ask yourself what you can change?

The ability to adapt it's a sign of inner power, self-strength; however, being flexible is another key in your path to success.

Your subconscious mind is a fantastic engine that, if accessed and used intentionally, will propel you rapidly closer to the life and goals you desire and, most importantly, to the ones that match who you are, your identity.

Tell me, what is the most important thing in your life?

Family, career, health, relationships, Social Life?

What is your biggest dream?

Is your dream related to your number one priority?

Compile a "dream list" of those things you want to manifest into your life, then give each one a month of the calendar.

Make a list of things that work easily and things that you need to do differently.

The Known and The Unknown

Many things connect people: love, common interests, benefits, profits, disasters, addiction, social class, hobbies, much of it hate, and the list goes on, but if we can connect in gratitude, then we have gained the liberty to live authentically with joy and fulfillment.

See that bird? It's a brown-throated thrush, but in Germany, it's called a halzenfugel, and in Chinese, they call it a Chung ling, and even if you know all those names for it, you still don't know anything about the bird.

You only know something about people; what they call the bird. Now that thrush sings and teaches its youngest to fly and flies so many miles away during the summer across the country, and nobody knows how it finds its way. -" Richard Feynman".

So, you think you know someone?

Just because you know his/her name or because you spent some time together and had some meaningful conversations, do you think you know someone?

Deep inside, we are someone who no one else has even met, yet we want to be loved and understood for that. The art of controversy!

Let's scroll back a little; you think you know someone when you don't even know yourself?

We do hide even deeper inside as people act like they already know the best or worst of us, and what's the point of even trying to explain something we can't always explain to ourselves.

Trying to describe what we do well hiding from ourselves, how to describe with words as who we are and what we like, and how we think or what we love when we alone struggle to understand when we begin and when we stop hiding from ourselves.

So, I will ask again: You think you know someone? But do you know yourself?

Everything twitches when you get to know yourself; you begin to understand how easy someone changes and how hard it is to change. How easy it is to assume you know and how complex it is to know someone else.

We live in times where people assume more than explore, where people simply decide they know someone else; they figure out others.

We have been disciplined on what and how to think, yet we have never been taught how to break free from predetermined ideas and let the unknown and absolute reality and the personal truth sink in.

In the same way, we observe ourselves while we search for inner wisdom, we have to follow the same approach when we meet others.

Start to know people without deciding that you already know them truly. Have you ever confidently and in absolute truth said: I know me completely, and there Is nothing new I can learn about myself? I think not!

Well, the very same applies to knowing others, we don't really know them until they let us in, and to get access to knowing them deeply, it takes interest, commitment, curiosity, respect, and no assumptions whatsoever.

We assume we know; we state that we know; we believe that what we learn about others is the actual truth, and we start to misjudge and misconceive ideas.

If we start from, "I don't really know that person, but I would love to, and I am ready to give the same amount that I want for someone to give me before branding me", then you reach the first step into someone else's reality.

The first step is to ask yourself: **Who am I? What do I see in others?** It's all part of strategic thinking.

1. Who am I?
2. What do I want?
3. What do I like?
4. What do I need?

5. What do I love the most?
6. Why do I love what I love the most?
7. Where am I going if I do this or that?
8. Who do I want to be?
9. Why do I want to be that?
10. What do I want out of this or that, and always why? Always have you're why, your what, and your how connected.

Our mind gathers up information every day, which entails important and non-important details. Now depending on how receptive we are, the state of our mind at that given moment, we process the information, and based on that, we decide to retain and use them in our everyday lives. This is basic functioning.

Our subconscious mind is picking up information after information. It repeats this every day, and that is being influenced by our environment, surrounding, or whom we spend time with, and so on.

Can you consider the amount of information our predecessors received daily compared to the amount we receive today? So incomparable, isn't it? No wonder you find it hard to have a clear vision, and you lose your focus often, and even at times, everything seems foggy.

Discipline- The answer is to slow down, decide what is important, select the type of information you need to process, and ensure that you select your thoughts the same way you choose your clothes and other things you select intentionally every day.

We all know what to do; the challenge is in how to get ourselves to do what we need to do, and I am not talking here about the basic needs even though some fail to do that.

The key is to create the mindset and build the discipline to support you in the process and in the way you talk to your mind about why you need to be doing what you should be doing to get you to what you need to be.

1. Mindset (decide what you want, why you want)
2. How?
3. Create the discipline
4. Separate what you need from what you want
5. Make a list of things you can't control related to your what and why
6. Make a list of things you can control and also do easily related to you what and why
7. Make a list of Impossible (they all turn into possible eventually).

We are the only creatures that have the capacity to think while we are thinking. So use that for your improvement.

Strategic Thinking

The ability that will advance you rapidly from your start to your finishing line is the goal.

Who are the three most important people you admire the most, dead or alive? What is the quality you admire the most, and what skills do you want to master as much?

Reconsider the abilities, skills, qualities, and then select one role model that covers the most, study, and acquire as much information possible. Chose three main skills and master those.

Being a Winner with Blind spots

We mostly desire things that are far out of reach, and while we don't always get what we want, however when we do get them, we tend to ignore them and look for things we do not have again.

We love the unobtainable, the untouchable, the challenges because we are ambitious driven. While this is a good thing, the downside is that we can't really enjoy what we already have and what we so hardly obtain we start looking for new items. So I utterly encourage you to look ahead and far reach, but I also recommend the reader stop, breath into the present moment while measuring how far we've come, all as a sign of celebration that is vital in our progress.

Remember the things you have now, and you don't enjoy as you should or thought you would? Those things are what once upon a time you could only dream of.... A job, a car, a family, a business...a performance, etc.

The entire meaning of desire, of making things happen for ourselves, the point of being a winner, is to enjoy every bit of our achievements and enjoy the experiences we encounter in the way of touching the untouchable.

Of course, the goal is to see the top of the mountain, but the primary purpose is to see, enjoy, acknowledge, feel: nature, the trees, the flowers on the way to the top. I know, easier said than done. So please, dream and desire what is far-reaching, and while you pursue with baby steps but in complete confidence, you need to be fully present in the way of achieving.

We often ignore our winnings completely as we regard them as small or insignificant because we achieve them easily. And are unaware that those small winnings are the steps towards the bigger winning.

What creates the difference in someone's life is what they dream of, what they desire, why, and how they go after what they want for themselves.

Competitive People love to know; they love to feel that they are ahead of others, that they have an aspect of their life they master better than others, ahead of the ones they feel competitive with, or considered to have it all sorted out.

We become the people we spend time with, we become the books we read, the tv channels that we watch, we become the accounts that we follow, and most certainly, we become what we constantly think of, what we constantly identify ourselves with, what we think of becoming.

We become what we admire, what we crave for, what we like, what we focus on.

Think of this: we are what we eat, drink, sleep and hear. We are our habits, our constant doing; we are what we constantly think of and create our movements that become our actions. Our actions are our responsibilities only, and they become the quality of our life.

Your support, resources, help, and personal power are in the first and last moments of your day. It is like a cup of coffee that energizes you. Thoughts are the major factor influencing your day; they are your everything. Your cup of energy!

Now, no less important: who's cup are you filling?

"Habit is either the best of servants or the worst of masters". *Nathaniel Emmons*, which means it either helps you grow or give you dependency and stagnation.

Habits and consistency, how many times have we heard about these two?

The only limit to the realization of tomorrow is your habits and your doubts of today.

If you build a healthy habit, it's only through consistency that you will have value or obtain valuable outcomes.
Eating healthy one day is ok; the value comes from consistency, eating healthy every day.

Just a quick example for the reader, you, **The Unstoppable You**.
We want to create results, and we want to have that always, not every now and again. What successful people and high performers have in common is consistency, which can be achieved only with laser focus and attachment to the outcome.

Opportunities: Creating Opportunities!

It is doubtful that someone else will show you opportunities for exactly, and I mean here exactly the things or the life you want for yourself. Manifesting is cocreation.

Let's analyze here and define opportunity: "*Opportunity*" a favorable timing, space, place, proximity, a moment that makes it possible to accomplish a certain thing or make it possible for you to grow towards the desired result: an advantage, a chance, good timing aligned with your existing goal.

Opportunity types: proximity, timing, network-related, coincidental, intentional.

Qualities you need to seek in an opportunity: rare, attractive, timely, adds value to your existing goal or need.

Now, how do we create opportunities? Over the years, I created opportunities for myself, the people I care about, and the clients I worked with. I can confidently state that opportunities are circumstances that we can create to our best advantage.

Imagine a job that pays well, and it's not hardcore exhausting. In order to get that, you need to create opportunities. Easier said than done, but it all starts with having said out loud what type of opportunity you want in your present time.

Let's remember: Network, proximity, and timing. The job is already yours.

Ask, and you shall receive, which means first you have to know what you want, then ask, and receive what you ask for.

YOUR NOTES

Chapter 4

Changing Your Identity

Identity

Establishing Habits (Patterns and identifying Limiting Beliefs)

Pillars

Self Portrait: The story you have been telling yourself and how you talk yourself out of doing things, we are more prone to find "why's " for why we are stuck rather than "how" we can get out of a situation and find better perspectives.

Rationalization: What is the defense mechanism you're creating to justify your habits or controversial behavior in a very seemingly rational, logical manner, so you avoid the truth or the fears.

Let's stop here for a minute and discuss patterns:

What are Patterns? Patterns are habits that serve us and habits that don't serve us. For example, if you bite your nails a few times, it will become a habit; you will do it automatically, so you have created a habit.

Likely, you did it once, created a pattern without even knowing, and then you did it again and again without realizing it every single time.

Clarity is power, so recognize patterns. Rituals define us, so it's important to establish your rituals so they can serve your desired identity.

Patterns + Decisions = Identity (who you are) or who you push yourself to be

Example of patterns addiction: certain emotions, criticism of yourself or others, food, sweets, alcohol, superficiality, clubs, porn, etc.

Detachment by strengthening your positive patterns, understand how you decide to cut upfront.

Let's rate yourself on a scale of 1 to 10:

Fear

Stress

Not being good enough

Financial status

All this creates a belief system as a coping mechanism. Describe each one.

Now, if you scale yourself 5, you have 50% space to grow and a 100% chance to become the best possible.

Changing bad habits and unfavorable patterns is not optional; what you're not changing, you're accepting as a fact and eventually become your reality. Your most robust drive is not necessarily serving you. You can argue for your limitations really strong as long as you have strong limiting beliefs, negative patterns, and a toxic mindset.

We are animalistic by nature, and that is a side we tend to overlook as we seek to avoid pain and chase pleasure.
Therefore, we procrastinate, we avoid clarity, we let ourselves be driven by toxic desires, and we self-sabotage".
Our rituals define us.

Pillar in growing: Curiosity, finding your What, Understanding your What, Excitement, Motivation, Discipline, A big Why to your What.

What: What would you want or love to do and understand that, get excited about knowing and understanding your what, keep yourself in that passionate state, discipline your steps, know why is that you want to do that, and ensure is of value to contribute to a better world. No matter how small the world it might be in that case.

YOUR NOTES

Chapter 5

Processing Changes: Adapting the Old to The New

Progress is impossible if you always do things the way you always do things; change, the diversity of how we are doing something, initiates, sustains progress, and, most importantly, creates an innovative personality.

To accomplish the life you want for yourself, you have to initiate change and embrace discipline; you have to do things you never considered yourself capable of or never considered doing. Don't confuse consistency with the need for change.

Temporary deviation with a post from Social Media:
CEO of Nokia ended his speech during the press conference to announce NOKIA being acquired by Microsoft by saying:

"We didn't do anything wrong, but somehow, we lost."
With this said, the entire management team, including himself, cried. Nokia was a respectable company. They have done nothing wrong with their business, but quickly, the world has changed. In fact, they have done the only thing they could have done wrong, they didn't

initiate change, they didn't take the decision, and they did not embrace new changes.

They missed out on learning and change, so they lost a valuable opportunity that was within reach for them to remain a giant entity in the market.

Not only did they miss an opportunity to grow more and faster, but they also lost their chance to survive!

The message from this story:
If you do not change, someone else will definitely create change, and you will dissolve into their changes; you may follow, but you will never lead.

If you do not want to learn new things and your thoughts and mentality cannot catch up with time, you will end up with time!

A person remains successful as long as he learns, and if he thinks he has learned enough and ignores new ways and change, he's condemning himself to failure.

Beliefs + Change +Decisions = Results
We need to create healthier beliefs, so we conduct our decisions by a healthy belief system that serves us, and therefore you create the most desirable results.

Now you need to look at your beliefs and patterns, preferences versus existing ones.

I had wonderful, talented people like my clients who came to me with all the wrong beliefs; even though they were doing well in some aspects of their lives, they were lacking so much in others.

Now let us understand the level of your existing potential from 1 to 10, and if you scale 5, you have to take five scale action.

A healthy belief example is: where I am is not who I am, my identity is who I am, so I have to strengthen my identity.
Of course, you have to begin with strengthening your patterns and habits.

Have you often heard the expression "force of habit"? Well, habits are a force that creates and shapes your identity and creates a life for you and not a life you want.

Anything worth doing in life takes risks, and the key challenge is to turn fear into motivation.

Instead of feeling afraid of taking that risk, connect to the end result, e.g., If you decide to change, but you're afraid, you have to be willing to change more than the fear itself.

Your inner dialogue should sound like this: I am willing to change into something I have never been, into the person that can get me to where I want and take the risk of failure, of not being comfortable, of losing people along the way, of getting into an absolute unknown.

Refusing to initiate changes in your personal journey is akin to accepting your self-professed failure as a continuous state of being. Refusing to initiate change will eventually make it impossible for you to adapt to the changes around you. While you can't control the outside facts in a constantly changing world, you can influence your outside world by initiating the changes you need within yourself.

Decades ago, I resented any type of change.

So, I found myself in great difficulties coping with the changes around me, even though I was changing as much as the outside world by refusing to accept, understand, learn about the inner changes (internal improvements). As a result, I was only creating difficulties in my personal growth.

Change and the past:

Think of your past like a tunnel without really being in front of you but rather something you leave behind while you go through and still carry around: you see it, you've been through, you embrace it, you accept it happened, and you come to realize that you had to go through these experiences for you to become the person that gets you where you are today, and the person you become today, the strengths you develop will now support your vision to become whoever is that you want to become.

The only evidence of what you become is from looking back at your past (the tunnel) and visioning the strengths you developed from there to here. You've changed; you can see the change, and in the same way, in the future, those changes you are about to make will be the tunnel you envision.

You have created change, inevitable, and you can measure it by looking into your personal past.

Accept, embrace and move into the now, and treat yourself as you already are the person you want to become.
Treat yourself like the person you want to become, and then the genius in you will act in ways as you become the person you want to become.

YOUR NOTES

Chapter 6

You and Emotional Beliefs

I remember this client of mine who came into my office and started by telling me how he was not concerned with the way he looked and that he accepted the way he was despite going to the extreme of repeatedly calling himself ugly.

He went on and on how and why he shouldn't care while his body, posture, and language contradicted everything he was saying. He created a self-image in his mind based on his assumptions of how others perceive him.

His posture and the way he carried himself told me how lonely he was and how much he longed for love, quality time, and emotional support.

What was the problem?

He refused to change and created the same behavior based on all the negative assumptions he could possibly make.

Body Language – old self -new self (describe the Posture of Old versus New)

Describe the old and new body language: posture, look, voice, speech, eating habits, etc.

It's how I decide that I am that matters the most.

Your level of worthiness can be set only by your behavior, and your behavior is set by your identity, who you think you really are.

What you are not changing in yourself, you accept it as true, as your own identity.

Your movements create your reality, and here I am not referring to actions but to the way you move every day and feel about yourself.

Body language, e.g., Pay attention to your contradictions, posture, tone of voice to certain situations, moments, the way you touch or hold things, how you react to people or situations.

The keys here are: Physical behavior, your expressions, the way you look, move and react is your non-verbal behavior and more likely is instinctively (habits, patterns) rather than consciously.

These keys show what your think of yourself, your level of worthiness, efficacy, and confidence. In a word, it shows who you think you are.

Self-image creates your reality, so if you see yourself as presentable and pleasant, others will eventually perceive you the same way.

Short deviation: Confidence

Confidence is typically regarded as a personality trait and the most powerful tool and admirable quality as it is not always easy to achieve.

The ones who struggle with self-confidence most likely have a set of limiting beliefs about life and how they can or should be. These types of constraining beliefs and the consequent false narrative allow anyone to distort or twist self-perception and concept of life.

Psychologist researchers say that these limiting thoughts are a product of our belief system, which starts developing in early childhood. They mean to say that from early life, we start to build a belief system of our own based on our immediate interactions, personal experiences, major impacts, and how we actually interpret them.

On the other hand, what can look like exuberant self-confidence could be out of extreme parenting encouragement and high performances early in school.

I personally experienced a lack of self-confidence from a very early age. I have been constantly reminded how I am good for nothing and how I am too dark, too tall, too thin, too different, too naughty, too loud, or too quiet. So I guess that what I am saying is that it happens to many of us, and we speak a self-talk language on our own, and being able to change all the lacking in self-confidence, one needs to change his entire self-talk language.

To reframe our entire language, we need to learn the negative vocabulary we use and what type of vocabulary we use for what type of instances.
What are the major repetitive negative words we use and when we use them mostly?

The second will be to find an alternative word to replace the first one and to understand which type of word serves us the best, for example, instead, I am not good enough, and this is always happening to me, we can say: I am getting more resourceful, and these are only chances to improve.

When we hit a roadblock at something or in our profession, job, performances, or when we simply make mistakes, we end up worrying about our own ability to succeed in what we want or in our current roles. Then that leads us deep into the self-negative talk, and we start experiencing the impostor syndrome.

We have all encountered challenging situations throughout our lives with no exceptions whatsoever and have managed our ways forward. `The missing piece is to realize that your negative self-talk is not serving you and that stays in the way of healthy self-confidence that is by far a quality that leads you to personal success.

Self-motivating affirmations:

1. I am complete, and I can find all that I need within
2. I have all that it takes to move forward
3. I am learning and becoming more resourceful every day
4. I look great, and I am more than enough
5. I've got this, and I do well
6. I am unstoppable
7. I am so proud of how far I have come and how I managed myself
8. I learned so much, and I am still learning like everyone else around
9. I believe I can achieve exactly what I set out to achieve.
10. I Can and I will, end of story. This is my favorite one as I created and repeated to myself in my times in need.

In our introductory coaching session, we start by observing the person that sits in front of us; the same goes in our everyday encounters.

When we observe someone, we pick information about their choices and who they decided to be or how they want to be perceived. While at times we assume things might not be real, we have to play a game of elimination in our mind and ensure we gain clarity from the volume of information we take in.

Your brain is designed to help you obtain what you want; your mind has a filter that allows what type of information your brain will process further and which of the information will be denied access into your brain.

Who you become is who you meant to become!

Being alive comes with endless possibilities. You can make any number of interesting things happen by willingness.
You can write words that become sentences on a piece of paper that will trigger certain thoughts later for you or someone else.

You can touch a few buttons on your phone and be speaking to any of a hundred people you know, and whatever is said would change each other's day, or life, in some way.

You could clean the house this afternoon or leave it messy, and each option would give a different shape to the evening.
Now tell me how wisely you chose your options?

YOUR NOTES

YOUR NOTES

Chapter 7
Why!

Your why! Value, what value do you give to what you do

Find out why you do what you do, and you will find your Why! As humans, we can adapt our mind almost to anything as long as we understand our own "why".

Everything is important but most important is to understand why you do what you do and find Your Why!

Once you are certain of your "why " you can establish new opportunities for your why and find ways to show up more in your why.

What is that you're emotionally connected to? Why? Your strongest reason for doing what you do is your highest level of motivation, which is your ticket to personal freedom, success, happiness.

Your why should connect your mind to an end result.

Our questions determine our path in life, the quality of our questions shapes our destiny. What we seek begins to seek us only when we start questioning everything around us and ourselves.

Words are the final touch that decides the quality of our experiences and ultimately influences our state, our emotions. Words are thoughts, and thoughts are words, and together they become milestones in our realizations.

Build your own supportive mastery vocabulary based on your why and wants, if you will, as that might get you easier to start. Connect your very own words to the experiences wisely and be very selective of your own thoughts. Make it a game, if you will, and be sure you master it. You can simply write this game by writing the twenty most positive common words and practice inclusiveness in your daily vocabulary.

Every second it's a new second, but you know that
Every moment it's a new moment, and you feel that
Every thought you create it's a new thought out of an old one
Every day it's a new day out of an old and followed by a new one
Every opportunity arises from old ashes of hopes that will sprinkle and glitter with joy your existence
Every smile is an old grimace turned into joy, a smile that becomes a unique kindness to a random source
Every rain it's a new endure that you get to feel with a new emotion
Every act of love is a new poem of expressing a new kind of love
Every breath that you take it's a new breath that becomes old
Every question you raise becomes a new path

Every day that you have a chance to experience becomes an old day tomorrow into a new one
Everything you are is a new you out of an old self and a new chance to enlighten yourself.

YOUR NOTES

Chapter 8
Seasons

Your winter shapes your springs, and your self-awareness shapes your winter.

Easy times make people weak simply because they do not need to grow.

Weak people generate bad situations because they're simply unprepared.

Tough times build strong people because they learn and evolve through difficulties, and we all know that strong people create Great Times.

While most of us focus on conquering the outside world, on how to make it big, how to succeed, it is in understanding our personal inner world that we create empowerment.

You are living a life that you have created unintentionally, so you might as well create intentionally a life that you enjoy living.

How?

Inner world: The power of self-awareness. (the power of self-knowledge, understating your feelings, what motives you, your desires, etc.).

The hardest winters are always followed by breathtaking springs. In the harsh seasons, you look deep inside and find every answer, every resource, every brilliant idea.

In the winter, we prepare to shine by growing stronger through adversity. The key is to acknowledge the toughest times as challenges rather than struggles, and life is not in adapting alone but in growing skills, knowledge, and habits while we adjust.

Internal Self-awareness has the remarkable ability to examine your thoughts, feelings, and emotions without being controlled by them. As a result, internal self-awareness helps you manage anxiety, depression, and stress more assertively and increases your focus.

External Self-Awareness is the ability to understand how others perceive you, simply said, understanding how others view us.

The external awareness helps you become socially more empathetic, consider the opinions of others, engage more deeply in meaningful conversations. Etc.

Self-Awareness is a skill no one is ever born with, and it's an ability that you develop and strengthen throughout your life.
It provides emotional stability, better interactions with others, more rationality, and fewer bad habits.

You can activate, improve, and develop your level of self-awareness by reading, exposing yourself to unfamiliar experiences, meditation, some yoga, being honest and transparent with what you want in life, having a mentor, doing right by others, and always doing so the best you can.

The self is constantly changing; it is essential to be aware of that and use it purposefully.

YOUR NOTES

Chapter 9

Your Personal Perception

The art of understanding negativity, fear, and how to include gratitude

Understanding emotions, thoughts, and feelings is a powerful tool and are art. The ability to comprehend what is really important, to select priorities, to be thoughtful, grateful is the path to endless possibilities.

Your level of perception and understanding will skyjack your way to success and deliver results. So, you see here "why" understanding is an art?

For some people, we all have the same nervous system, neurons, organs, capacity of endurance, etc.; for some people, these are stronger because they use the power of understanding.

What we believe is either a way of limiting ourselves or growing stronger and better ourselves in ways that serve us best. However, I don't mean you simply should be fearful; when you are afraid, you are not grateful, and if you are not grateful, your level of perception reduces to none.

If you follow the trail of your stress, it leads you to your fears. The fear of not being enough, not being able to make it, fear of not being lovable, fear of failing, we all have at least one of those fears as we are all subconsciously functioning under the same human basics.

Knowledge is power; understanding how to utilize your knowledge in your favor is the most powerful asset. Having this kind of high-frequency power is ultimately decisive in the quality of your life and your personal contribution.

Imagine all of the knowledge produced season by season, decade by decade, through centuries left to waste instead of contributing to the evolution of mankind and instead of being used for the benefit of each brilliant mind that actually understood that knowledge is powerful once you make use of it.

Imagine reading and reading, and over the years and over a life span, you continue to read, but you do nothing with all the information and knowledge you acquired over the years, or simply imagine a higher degree graduate with a complete set of knowledge practicing nothing and simply not tapping all the knowledge into some actions.

The first step in creating something great for yourself is to realize that success and failure are both totally and utterly dependent on you and are both equally scary.

I have been dreaming of sharing my thoughts forever with the world, with you, my lovely reader, ever since I can remember, and yet it's been and still is one of my biggest fears. I jumped out of a plane, and it wasn't that scary; I did things that other people put aside for life, yet the scariest thing on earth for me was, and it still is, to have everyone's attention on me. *Success

''Look at me'', smiling while facing my biggest dream and my biggest fear simultaneously.
Yes, success and failure are equally scary; combined, they will propel you to heights you can't even imagine.

Justification of your failures, justification of being in the same spot you are?

How do you justify being where you are? We all have a story we tell ourselves that either keeps us trapped or gets us going.

What does it cost you to make the move that you need to do?

What does it cost you not to make a move, to be in the same space?

It's hard for someone to overcome the power of a habit as that habit is being conditioned by years of practice and that deep belief that is unchangeable.

Engineering your intention to change is something that will rock your personal world filled with patterns and habits. Understanding and stating clearly that you have a negative habit of eliminating that habit by replacing it with a constructive one is what I mean by engineering your intention to eliminate, change, or simply strengthen the healthy, valuable habits.

Pain. Your pain should be your fuel, and your drive should be your anchor.

When in pain, disdain, confusion, sorrows, or depression, our feelings are very strong and overwhelming. They will make you think and say things about yourself, the worst possible things you could.

You will deliberately sabotage yourself even more into that negative state of mind, more likely unknowingly, all that while you know, you will delay your way out.

Because at times, there is a sweetness in that pain(the familiar), in thinking that you own it and that you are the only one that deals with it and understands it.

I know of a lifetime battling life, pain, the feeling of rejection, failure, confusion, anxiety, depression, struggles, loneliness especially. I have experienced emotional pain, and I can tell you that it feels as hard if not harder than a broken bone, but as much as the body heals, the emotional part of the brain heals too eventually.

The challenge is with the scars; the emotional scars are different than the physical scars as they can open wide if triggered and when least expected. So how do you heal a broken heart when you have no emotional support?

You give your pain a meaning; you turn it into wisdom; you add it to a purpose.

Your pain, your trauma make you strong and not otherwise. You turn your pain into a driving force, and the gap is finding your ultimate goal.

I've gone to bed with pain, disarray, and loneliness and had to drag myself out of the darkest spaces; my mind went hiding, but I am no ashamed of that as I am standing here with a purpose: To uplift you, to encourage you, to be your, Captain, your Leader for hope.

I want you to stand up for yourself the same way I do now in my mind while writing this to you, my beautiful reader, and repeat to yourself:

I (name) Elena Monica stands here today to say in all openness:
That this is ME, a loving force of the universe with broken feathers pieced together so I can heal your broken wounds and put the hopes back in your heart where it belongs.

In my times of loneliness, I searched for someone like me, and in my times of pain and disdain, I looked to find someone like me, and here I am, all pieced together as I find myself.

CLIENTS and their Hidden Stories

People judge according to their needs, and that is called limitation.

I had clients who were so protective of their negative situations that they could vehemently contradict every attempt to change and justify with ease why they did it. So people are very protective of their own limiting beliefs, and behind that is not always trauma but the fears they get attached to, which they developed throughout their lives until this day.

I had a client originally from Jordan with a very pleasing personality, extremely likable at first glance that I named Mr. Eventually But, as for every new insight, input, suggestion, discovery, possibility to improve, he immediately responded with: "but Monica, this and that"…. He will always put so much energy into justifying why this or that might not work that he was in complete denial of how things could have turned better.

What was wrong with his approach?

One needs to focus on the possibilities for success and not on the chances of failure! The healthiest approach is to look for ways out and not why you are stuck in the first place; this becomes secondary as a lesson to learn and a failure to avoid.

And I had a Scottish client that every single conversation will repeatedly emphasize how idiotic and what assholes people are and how he was not having enough. I am sure somehow, he was right because he was most probably perpetuating the same type of experiences with that kind of attitude in mind. Although he was secretly asking for compliments and appreciation, he would victimize himself in all instances and situations.

I had a couple that I worked with, and while she has a very constructive mindset and behavior, he was in complete denial and a negative state of mind.

Everything and everyone was wrong and against his expectations, and of course, he was looking at the world with the feelings and wants produced by these personal thoughts. I knew deep inside in the subconscious mind while in complete denial that he was failing his wife, himself, and everyone he was in contact with. Everything had a negative story, and there was no beauty or positive in anything.

Another client of mine came to me saying that she is not feeling good enough unless she gets external validations, and while she seems to have it altogether deep inside, she was one of the most insecure people I ever met. It is important here to keep in mind that she had a brief background in psychology, and she led a life that seemed perfect to the outside world and looked like she had it all together.

Her reasoning was that she was in search of passion and true connection. We worked together, and while no trauma was there, there was a child who has developed a narcissistic personality that needed to be fed constantly. Imagine this pretty woman who was one of the prettiest when I met her the first time, turning into all kinds of esthetic interventions that disempowered her beauty.

We have successfully freed her of her insecurities and treated her narcissism but only after agreeing and accepting she was suffering from those patterns.

Another client of mine and I have to emphasize here that she was a gorgeous tall young lady that was professionally accomplished and her main problem was that she wasn't happy in her own skin and she couldn't feel beautiful although she knew from others and the mirror that she was.

In his early sixties, a well-established Swiss business owner came to me and, with the arrogance of a self-made well-accomplished business owner, simply demanded of me: here I am, now tell me what's wrong with me.

He was clearly unhappy but so used to covering up and saving the appearances that he couldn't get to the bottom of it, and while he said that his main problem is landing and being in a healthy committed relationship, he wanted variety; he wanted to be pitched, he was extremely pretentious and wasn't willing to offer much in return. He was lying to himself and every woman he would come in contact with.

I remember a very complicated, intelligent Irish client of mine came to me and said he was divorcing his wife after having four children.

He blamed his wife for everything and even because she worked out and kept fit while he was more like a grizzly bear. His main concern was how to ensure he could keep their 'estate' (his exact words) for his children and get a wife that could take him in his very late fifties and without a penny to his name, but in return give him finances to maintain the 'estate' and his children.

He said he wanted no more children and had no desire to make efforts on his look, no generosity, and wanted a woman that could love him for exactly what he is. So you see how twisted his self-made story was, and he was proud to own that kind of complication.

As we worked together to help him gain clarity in his new venture, I sat there listening in complete astonishment describing his future type of woman, and I couldn't hold myself wondering how far he would go with shocking me. He taught me a lot through his variations.

He said, and I quote, the women I want to rebuild my life with must simply like me the way I am and not expect me or ask me to change. But, of course, he didn't want a clingy kind of needy woman, and of course, he dreamed of a dreamy woman just for him to like him just the way he was. A constant negative complainer is frustrated and so unfit that he defied the term unfit. He is still single and only hired to help him make decisions related to whereabouts in his professional choices.

A retired Austrian client of mine came to me because he felt insecure and lonely, and after an early in life divorce and a long-term relationship, both ended against his will, and he wanted to find the woman of his dreams.

We love people because they make us feel better about ourselves, some because they make us feel superior or simply put, important.
Some because we feel better about the choices that we make, some because of the opportunities they create for us, and mostly because we have the chance to love.

And then again, If we are not ready to love, we are not going to receive that love, only to find out that what we perceive to be out there for ourselves is not what we could have had; and this is for my client that couldn't trust anyone and stayed in that safe place for as long as he could remember.

Accepting who you are doesn't mean you don't have to change who you are. This means I accept I am not good enough and that I can improve, so I need to change my perception to do so and become more than enough. That's what I work on with my clients.

As we progressed with the sessions, we realized his personal insecurities and fears of committing to a relationship. Like the previous client in this chapter, he kept saying he had nothing to offer to a woman, but he had a complete list of how his women should look, must walk, talk, and behave.

The main and only reason I divulge these stories with you here is to provide you with a vivid understanding of how far and the length some people go, only to deny the obvious and to cover up what they feel deep inside and know to be the truth. I want the reader to see the diversity of instances where we design the perfect blind spots for ourselves. The self-sabotage and hiding behind statements can make us arrogant and stuck in a negative state without much hope.

The more we avoid addressing our problems, the bigger they become. I've helped thousands of people throughout my life and in my career as a coach, but I couldn't have done it if they didn't want the change, f they didn't realize firsthand that something was wrong and it needed to be addressed. It goes pretty much in this sense: I don't like my job, financial status, location, how I feel about myself, my loneliness, my social status, my relationship, my circle, how I look etc etc etc….

What do I do?

I seek help, professional help, a therapist or a professional coach, someone who can see through me and relate to my story and my struggles. It has to be someone that cares enough to see my pain, struggles, or encourage me to become who I so much want to become.

Sweet self-sabotage, sweet arrogance and comfort zone, the whisper of I know it all, or there is nothing that can be done, this is how my life is and how someone can understand or make it all better. I just describe how easily we can sabotage every chance we have to succeed with the power of thinking. Admission, acceptance of who we are and letting go of the guilt without becoming arrogant, and all that will happen with the proper professional help.

What is the story you tell yourself about yourself or someone else that you blame or give excuses for being stuck the way you are and where you are right now?

You know how they say that you should be surrounded by only high-quality people etc. etc. etc.... and if you do that you will become the sixth one? Well, some people will choose people with the same vices, same habits, and people that can constantly approve and compliment them, and that is as well a form of self-sabotage.

We have fear, arrogance, and expectation without giving anything in return; we use people and turn up fearing they intend to use us.

We fear what we become, and we hurt people with the exact things that we fear the most, and most of the time, the people we end up hurting are the ones that indent and mean well. This is because we are so accustomed to judging the world around us that we don't see that we become the traits and patterns, the people and characteristics we judge the most.

Don't blame the weather; it rains on the rich as well. They get the sun; we get the blues; they get the blues; we get the sun; the joy is an unfaithful mistress. Life is constantly changing, though people's challenges don't change over time. We face similar challenges as our predecessor. What changes in our mind, and if we understand how to be in control of that, we can tap into the richest potential.

I realized that being forced to look for solutions at times instead of blaming the weather, the life, government, the partner, etc., made me tap into my potential and reach the most desirable results.

For example. After my divorce. After I cried for a while and after I stopped blaming him and myself, I started to focus only on what I could do to become stronger, regain self-confidence, trust, become a smarter version that can make things happen for herself. You will eventually find better ways when you intentionally look for better ways. It is the way your mind channels and is where your mind constantly goes that your energy goes to. You think positive, your energy will be positive, of I can Make it attitude.

If you're thinking negatively, then you know how it will go...

It is the attitude and the intention of your attitude that will deliver you the desired outcome.

Don't wait until you are ready to start, or you might never start; start with what you have or only your attitude.

So, if you constantly look for ways to improve and succeed at something, then your entire energy will produce solutions for that. Now, the question remains how to find what you are looking for? While I don't know what you could look for in life and what your heart desire is, I know that if you know what you want, the rest is a matter of methodology, planning, persuasion, resources, and follow-through.

The hardest part is not achieving but deciding what you want to achieve and actually enjoying what you have achieved. We live in the shadow of our own imposed limitations.
Who would you be without limitations, constraints, fears, the tendency to victimize yourself?!

We are perfect living creatures, yet we doubt the most and live in fear the most.

YOUR NOTES

Chapter 10

Fear

Think of fear this way: you have survived every single thing you thought you wouldn't survive, so do a constant reminder to yourself: everything you want is on the other side of fear.

The fear of making "the wrong decision" can paralyze people into years of indecisiveness, unfulfillment, and animosity. Yet, facing our fears, challenging our fears and worries is part of growing and creating personal success.

Our fearlessness shall be our secret weapon. "John Green"

I remember Claudia, a client I worked with, and that inspires this chapter, and as I do, I am sending her my thoughts of gratitude. She stepped into the coffee shop that we both agreed to meet over the phone, looking bright and assured, and as she sat down, I could tell she had some concerns and fears she wanted to share with me.

We had a great connection right from the start, and as she started talking, I simply couldn't help thinking how this woman in front of me could have such a timid voice while over the phone, and at first glance, she looked so assured. As she started talking to me and as I listened to her words, my main understanding was that she feared making a change in her personal life and career.

How do you know when it's time to *"make a decision"*, when it's time to *"take a leap of faith"* and leave something behind, a life you made for yourself but is not fulfilling, a house, someone or how do you know when you should give a chance to something new, a new place, a new relation, a new beginning, a new life.

Deciding when to move on from something can be overwhelming, and doing that from a place of fear or scarcity is not an easy leap but a giant step; giving strong meaning to what you want will create the emotion that will serve you in your path.

Giving a strong meaning to what you want will create the emotion that will aid and support your course and at times without feeling drained by the efforts you make.

At times we feel powerless when facing the moment of doing something effective with our lives. It takes real courage to get out of what we have been through and to exchange conformity of what we've been molded, and that is our comfortability to courage and discomfort. Conformity becomes fearfulness, and that will hold us back from achieving, from evolving, from succeeding, from taking our life to the next level, a level that we chose for ourselves and not that we conform to it.

How to decide from a place that serves you and not from the position where you think you have no choice, and from a place where you can bounce safely or simply explained: how to have your own back?

Our lives directly reflect our fear and directly result from our personal limitations, thoughts, and beliefs.

If you want better things, better relations, and better experiences in your life, you have to be very selective of what you choose to think and believe about yourself and what you choose to learn.

How much of your life you spent worrying or limiting yourself is crucially decisive of the life you are creating for yourself.

We all live the lives that we have created for ourselves, so why not consciously and in full power the best life we want for ourselves.

The fear of fraudulence, of not being good enough, these types of fears will empower your saboteurs. Eventually, you will deny your own ability, talents, skills, and opportunities, and you will do everything possible to confirm and approve of your fears and remain exactly where you are.

Fear of rejection will turn you into a fear of abandonment, and that fear of failure will turn into scarcity.

The chances are that you will turn into an introvert out of the fear of rejection; you will avoid trying new things at all costs. You will avoid relationships, commitments, attachment, and affection out of the fear of abandonment.

The fear of failure turns into scarcity and risk becoming extremely stingy.

The cycle: the comfort zone, worries, regressing, rejecting, limiting, deeper into the comfort zone and then your fears will elevate the anxiety state and the cycle starts over and over again and again, then eventually this becomes your patterns, your beliefs, your familiar state and you will begin to protect that will all your being.

Fear is not always keeping you safe is the opposite of safety when it comes to the matter of growth and can hold you hostage in the most unfavorable situation.

Fear is not the opposite of love; fear is the separation of love- the fear of rejection, abandonment, fear of commitment.

Fear is not the opposite of success but the house of failure if you decide to give it space into your life; fear is the house of failure if the fear of failing and the fear of criticism or not being perfect is greater than your desire to succeed.

Fear is like an alarm system that was once buzzing; you should "wake up" to see exactly' why" you fear and what you fear.

It is like when you look into your performance, writing, a photo, a job interview, a situation that didn't go quite well as you expected, this isn't good, and this is not the way I want it, but you avoid looking at that when in fact you need to look at it because it's your place to get your information and your only way to get it better.

Constantly do the things that terrify you the most (taking risks, spending time alone, taking time off, putting yourself out there). Overcoming your fears will help you gain a level of confidence that is so powerful and so empowering. I know people who overcome intimacy issues, insecurities issues, dependency issues by simply facing their own fears.

What things keep you in that same place or where you are and away from achieving the things you want and having the exact lifestyle you secretly crave? You might be scared of changes or getting even started, but I would rather be scared of not starting as this is the worst place to be and worst place to stay, anxious, frightened, scared.

The doubts, the fear, the courage, the ambition, desire, focus, all of that and more are either your ingredients for the failure of success. You're exactly what you think 99% of the time, meaning if you think of yourself as a poet, then go be a poet. Self-growth becomes impossible if you always do the same things, you know how they say it takes practice, well practice as well means repetition and repeating the same things will create a plateau, and you will get so comfortable with that that the need for change will be repressed and there you go, you got nothing.

Crisis creates or destroys a person, as the sense of fear will gradually fade away, and the sense of belief, strongly believe in your passion will become your state of mind.

Face your fears, change your surroundings, turn your life around.

YOUR NOTES

Chapter 11

Emotions

Emotions are clear messages; stop rejecting them out of fear. We actually make emotions that seem to happen to us; it is called subconsciously predicting. We predict the turn of the events right in front of us, and that creates a set of emotions.

We can have more control over our emotion by understanding how our mind works and how we actually predict the events in front of us.

Our emotions find their way out: we slam a door, we shout om traffic, we cry alone, we drink, we go to the gym, we have random sex, we get hooked by apps and social media platforms, we wake up early, or we lay in bed really late, we practice yoga, whatever is that we do our emotions finding their ways out.

We don't look at the way we slam a door but at the anger and the moment that triggered that expression of emotions. Imagine having just one song to cover your emotions, just a soundtrack for all the movies out there, just one-color shade for everything. That is how you have different triggers through different emotions for various reasons and needs.

Taking control of our repetitive emotions will positively impact how we influence our experiences' quality.

What is the consistent emotion your subconscious mind is creating? You master your emotion, and you master the quality of your own experiences.

Tools to influence your emotions:

1. Focus
2. Beliefs
3. Questions
4. Words
5. Rules
6. Values
7. Personal Identity
8. Goals
9. Dreams
10. Life Philosophy
11. Metaphors
12. Compelling associative vocabulary
13. Transformative self-talk
14. Environment

Journaling.
Create a list of repetitive emotions and the experiences that triggered these emotions for a week. Note it down every single day. Are those emotions empowering or disempowering emotions?

You can replace negative emotions with positive ones and create empowering imaginative experiences.

We all have similar experiences, good or bad; I can remind the reader here that our experiences are not unique, but the way we experience them is. With the right education in mind, it creates unique possibilities in our lives.

Without Formalities

At times we all believe we are at the finishing line, and we can start to rest, and then we suddenly realize that "resting" is not optional as we get pulled back right in the middle of challenges that creates stress, discomfort, and confusion. The biggest challenge to take on has the strength to continue against all odds, not losing yourself in the middle of your struggle instead of fighting your way to the real finishing line. A better version of yourself, equipped, completed, and accomplished…that your finishing line.

What is your finishing line?

How do you look?

What unique advantages do you have?

You see, my lovely reader, I might sound like a cliché, but that won't stop me from writing, and my finishing line is that I don't have a finishing line. I don't have a finishing line because I imagine myself always learning, always thinking in depths, perfecting, changing, adapting, and not doing more and new things as there is never enough time to have a finishing line.

However, if you ask me differently, like my biggest goal or where I want to reach, how far do I want to go, you change the narrative.

My biggest goal is YOU, to have inspired you to create the change you need, to impact your life even in the slightest mode but have taken you a step closer to that better self you need to be and to the quality of life that you desire and share that with someone you love.

I was born with a vivid dream that I was flying, I was floating over the world, and it was peace all around, and the vivid color of peach was holding me.

I came to be with you, my lovely reader.
I dreamed of love, affection, togetherness, understanding, and consideration as I lived every day of my everyday life craving love and affection. I was so troubled by its absence that I tried to run from love and life and even myself.

One day my dream came back to me, and I found love deep hidden in myself, and I was wiser, stronger, and grateful that I didn't give up, that I held onto the love inside of me and cherished it even when I was at my worst.

Relationships with self and others! Happiness and true self!

How else would you learn more about yourself by experiencing relationships of various backgrounds, cultures, religions, and beliefs? So embrace diversity, and in return, you will not only be accepted but you will be truly loved. What is life, after all, if not knowing more of what is that we are, the human nature, breaking someone's walls, healing their wounds, or even showering them with as much affection s they need and sprinkle that with the undeniable truth, we are emotional beings.

Everything heals with care and kindness; every relation can last with almost the same ingredients, but trust and empathy are the main ones.

I always suggest embracing solitude to learn and separate being alone from loneliness and neediness from loneliness. You know that being alone creates some sort of independence that becomes very addictive, but is powerful a definite way to learn about yourself, your true passion, calling, purpose, and matter of the heart. In solitude, we learn our deepest thoughts; we discover the true self, the being, and its importance.

Your fears reflect your expectations of fulfillment in a relationship! Commonly, our subconscious creates perfect ideals of true love; we aspire to meet that special one and be everything that special one needs, and we are prepared to compromise for that love, everything, and even so much in return for that love back. (naturally).

The problem is that nobody can complete us if we feel incomplete, uneasy, needy, and expect someone else to do that for us. No matter how much someone else loves us, all they can do is to love us through their own needs and emotions, so the feeling of being complete comes from and through self-love, self-knowing, and self-acceptance. Our partners can't complete us or deliver us fulfillment if that doesn't exist already within ourselves. All they can do is temporarily fill a void. No matter how hard or how much someone will try to do that for us and no matter how much we expect them to deliver that for us.

If we wish for someone to love us in a specific manner, it's because we have a need that we want to be fulfilled by someone else. These needs will create gaps that eventually influence our understanding of what love is and what relationship is about. These can only be adjusted by identifying the gaps as our own doing and our own responsibilities to, in fact, address them. If we examine ourselves, we usually find out that the source of all these expectations comes from what we miss the most emotionally in our lives, and in fact, the truth is that no one else can do that for us but ourselves.

Remember, we are more emotionally done logically; many will try to prove us wrong.

Let me explain further; for example, if we deal with the fear of loneliness or abandonment, we will be ok or even happy with someone simply because they give us a sense of security. If we deal with the belief that we are not good enough, we will settle for someone that simply validates us and feeds our ego, and all together, we will be happy only with a partner that we believe in filling that gap.

When our partner fills that void for us, we will feel like we are in the perfect relationship with the perfect soulmate, and we tell ourselves that we are complete because of that. Now, the danger comes in the times when our partner stops doing the work for us and stops filling the void for us. This is because people are continuously changing, as change is the biggest constant, and so we are our partners, lovers, soulmates, and they can't keep filling In the role we assign to them as the unattended void might get bigger.

As other people change, as we change as well, the voids get bigger and wider, and we end up wondering why we become so different. So we need to heal, and we need to fill those voids before we invite someone into our lives, before we invest ourselves emotionally and before we let our faith into someone else's hands.

Someone once asked me, as I also asked myself, why is it so wrong to believe that someone else can make us happy and complete us?

Why is it so wrong to believe that we can be happy only in a relationship? It is somewhat and somehow simply because happiness is not a constant state of being but often or not feeling that we find in ourselves triggered by emotions that we allow through some events or circumstances, and that is what we can share with a right fit so-called soulmate. This is completion but is not a continuity through a partner but within yourself.

To be happy or even content in a love relationship, we need to be happy on our own instead of searching for happiness through a relationship or marriage. Another person can trigger happiness, but we need to find it ourselves, on our own, and then share it with someone else who did the same.

Finding common sense and happiness.

As soon as we meet our basic needs and comfort, our lives become more about searching for purpose and happiness. The challenge is that we often get lost or turned around from our path, and we end up seeking without knowing what and with the belief that certain things will get us to that emotional state of happiness. We might get the things, but not necessarily the feelings we want.

We learn bitterness and disappointment as people turn out not to be who we thought they were, rejections and disappointments take place, and happiness starts to run through our fingers. Relationships sometimes become the source of emotional drama, insecurities, and heartbreaks.

Sacrificing time for much-envied careers, no passion present, and as we may work hard to accomplish our goals only to find out that we are empty and unfulfilled inside. We ignore the soul for temporary need and ignore the truth for temporary happiness. Eventually, we end up facing our demons, the demons we now must befriend to finally reach true joy.

Ignoring the soul is a quick suicide of our very own spirit. Eventually, even our body continues to live, our spirit ceases to exist, and we end up being merely an existence.

The road is finding Joy!
Taking time to evaluate your emotions, thoughts, and priorities can be really challenging, but this is just the beginning of a beautiful road.

Remember not the destination as much as the journey.

Awareness: Locate and change any false belief or limitation into a powerful one.

Work hard and develop personal willpower, a support system.

Always look forward with a positive mind, and change the old ways so you can shift to endless possibilities. This means that even if you don't know where you are going yet, trust the process and avoid any old ways that got you nowhere anyways.

Don't be afraid of people and never envy anyone, as every person hides a wound, a scar, a healed or unhealed wound. I had a few wounds myself, unhealed at the time and hidden so well that I didn't even know they existed for a very long time. People are not always likely to open up about their wounds; sometimes, they don't even know they carry them, which is like an anchor that keeps them in an unfavorable story or place and blocks the process. The same is for each one of us; we might carry wounds we don't even know we have.

Spending time alone, hiring a coach for your needs, reading, selecting and having a hobby, etc., endless possibilities that eventually will lead you to self-discovery.

YOUR NOTES

YOUR NOTES

Chapter 12

Facing Your Battles

Stop running after what you want and start attracting the right things in your life.

We become more powerful by focusing on producing the right thoughts, so your entire focus and question should go on how and never on when and why. Take control of your consistent emotions and consciously and intentionally shape your everyday life and the quality of your experiences.

One of my first clients, a guy named Omar who was in his late 30s, a pharmacist with great potential but recently divorced and looking for a new relationship, wanted to upscale his career. He felt invisible and unappreciated but mistreated at the same time. His problem was he wanted his way or no other way.

He would pick up conflict with his colleagues at the worst time and avoid conflict exactly when necessary.

His chances to change something in his current situation and be successful in his career was directly depended on his thoughts and emotions. He was so deep into it that he had an answer to contradict every professional suggestion that started with "but Monica" and eventually, I had a nickname for him, Mr. O, but. He would be in such a need to be right that he denied his own potential, chances, and possibilities.

I am sure he is doing better today, but at the time, it looked impossible for him to get out of the vicious cycle he created for himself, and the worst part was he would refuse to accept that he was the one that needed it to change, adjust, adapt, and transform his life into the most desirable ones.

The saboteurs, sweet self-sabotage that we indulge ourselves when times are tough and become the inner enemy that we are attached to it the same way we stick to unfavorable relationships.

Affirmation: *I am open to change and becoming who I need to become in order to create the results I want for myself.*

The results you have or not have, the life you lead now, are based on the decision you made, and you manage to grow because you, at times, were not satisfied with what you had or where you were and wanted more for yourself.

If you are a professional woman aged 30-50 who wants to create a wonderful shift in her life and become powerful on her terms, this book is written for "**The Unstoppable You**". This is your BOOK.

Self-esteem

Self-esteem is the most fundamental human need, and when it comes to today's fast-changing trends, as basic as this need, we all need to evaluate the level of our personal worthiness.

What is self-esteem?

It measures how we think about ourselves in relation to other people; it's our personal assessment compared to the people around us. Suppose you always imagine other people are better than you are. In that case,

Let me explain this way: if your level of self-esteem is low, you most likely really want to understand the cause if you haven't done it yet and gradually build a genuine self-trust. Your biggest expense in life is lacking self-confidence.

Second, that let's focus on insecurities:

1. Make a list, and as you go through it one by one, notice if they are old beliefs or part of your current identity; of course, I am referring to them as part of who you currently think you are, who you currently identify with a person. Some insecurities and beliefs start to build up early in life or are built due to circumstances or experiences later in your life. We know by now that self-esteem is vital in all aspects of your life.

2. Now, question yourself: who are these people that you compare yourself the most with, in such a way that you doubt your own skills, abilities, talents, your worthiness, your core identity. What do they have in common?

3. Now, make a list of qualities, things you believe about yourself that make you stand out, and a list of things you should do but can't because of your inner limitations. Understanding why you lack self-confidence is key, and I know you find me repeating that; I simply can't highlight it enough.
4. Make a list of people that you admire the most? Now, what do they have in common?
5. Make a list of the qualities that someone like you usually has. Then, again, make a list with your own attributes.

Too many lists? Nope, some words will be repetitive, and that is where your key answer is.

Causes: Most likely, if you were constantly criticized, bullied, insulted, treated with sarcasm, ridiculed or teased, and intentionally made to feel inferior, then you ended up absorbing those negative messages as true and started doubting your own abilities, your qualities, your beauty, your originality, your uniqueness.

A piece of worthy advice: Never fall into the trap of asking yourself why do they pick on you! They don't select, and this kind of experience happens to the best of us.

Let's go back and simplify even more: what is low self-esteem?

It's a false perception we have about ourselves and our general capabilities and or allowing someone else's perception to inflict into our subconscious mind.

General signs of low self-esteem: focusing more on failure than accomplishments, not accepting compliments as true, stating negative things about self, feelings sad, anxious or and depressed, ashamed, insecure, self-doubt, poor self-confidence, negative self-talk, and a great fear of failure, a constant need for comparison.

Common causes: Unhappy childhood, poor performances early in life, toxic environments, bad criticism from parents or siblings, teachers, colleagues, etc., an ongoing stressful life.

A lack of opportunities versus aspirations can influence low self-esteem, and the IMPACT can be "overwhelming".

Attitude: If you feel insecure, lack confidence in what you can achieve, of who you can be, if you feel like a failure, unloved, inadequate at times, and consistently afraid of making mistakes or fear of letting others down, then a complete change of mindset and an attitude makeover is long overdue now.

Find your inner strength, find your inner voice, relearn who you are.

YOUR NOTES

Chapter 13
Stand Still

Words are introductory; Steps are performances.
Aligning them is key.

Every attachment, possession, and relation are factors that create invisible side effects. Every little thing you feel, think and do creates invisible impacts on our choices and lives. Our attachments are more psychological, and so are our possessions; they are less physical and more psychological, but they are actively coexisting, and they affect our immediate environments. Please, please, please read it again.

People might not like you; people sure will not understand you at times, people will let you down when least expected, people will outsize you and mostly ignore you, criticize you, tell you or make you feel like you don't matter.

There will be times when you will be deserted by everyone around you and feel like you speak a language only you understand, and talking to a wall feels like the only way; please don't lose yourself to that. I promise you that if your intention is pure and you believe in the power of what you have to offer, you're going to get out of these rough times like the winner that you are. Stronger, kinder, and wiser. People often rely on what they shouldn't and couldn't and wouldn't on the behavior of others, and that creates internal negative stories that eventually surface in the rebellious forms and in self-sabotage while pushing them even farther from clear reality.

From opportunities, from the obvious, from what is available and within reach. What helps and keeps us firm from drifting or sailing dangerously far from shore (reality) is a rediscovery; let's, reestablish our values, our personal values, and no one else's indication, the exact individual needs that are in line with our personal values as they deliver the sense of personal fulfillment. The values are the food for thoughts and hidden emotional resources that can and will support us in making the healthiest and wealthiest decisions at any time.

Your personal values create a real sense of purpose, importance, clarity, direction, and determination. On the other hand, people create problems in their minds; they create negative thoughts.

They create problems in their minds and subconsciously maintain those problems as they get attached to them; they believe they are real and develop a sense of ownership. This is how people hypnotize themselves, and the good part of this type of behavior is that we can hypnotize ourselves for all the positivity and create joy and wealth instead.

Problems that can't be solved:

- The Inevitable passage of time or the aging
- Something that is already in the past and no one can change
- Something that is completely outside of your control, like the behavior of someone else, a virus, or the weather

These factors that are out of control can be very frustrating, moreover with the wrong mindset, sickening, disturbing, and creating anger base progress, and one can't base their personal happiness and success on them, of course.

There is an unrealized, unachieved need for love, importance, worthiness, or significance behind each of the problems we believe we have. Each of us individually has the power to decide and the power over what we choose; we need to make sure we make our decisions wisely and that they are ours and ours only.

The story we tell ourselves, the inner dialogue hypnotizes us, and we end up even feeling the pain of something that has never happened to us, and all that because whatever we constantly think of becomes real in our mind, whether it's true or false in reality. Having understand that we can take charge of our inner powers in creating the experiences that we want in our lives.

Stand still and stand for yourself first, my darling reader.

You need very little to start with, and that is the will, the mindset, and the discipline. The power of your own thoughts can become your best friends, best assets, valuable recourses, and limitless self-support.
In times like that, we have to decide what to do with the time that we have and who are the people that we want in our lives.

Only quality time and only quality people?

It makes sense, yet please remember your bad times and challenging experiences are the most instrumental lessons.

Treat yourself like the person you want to become, and the genius in you will act in the ways for you to become the person you want to become. Treat failures as lessons and treat everything in life with ease, and laser focus on the positive aspects of it.

I remember how little I used to think of myself, that I am not good enough, that I am not beautiful but ugly, that I don't matter, and I can't possibly be loved because being unloved and used was so familiar to me.

I was more comfortable with being rejected, so at ease that when someone was nice to me, I would always think they were there to use me, and mostly they were. I was always in search of love and validation, and as time passed by failure after failure, I became my own worst nightmare.

It doesn't have to be like that for anyone, and all I am trying to say here is that failure, pain, discomfort, scarcity, and rejection are the best teachers in life, the best advisors you can have when no one else is there.

I still remember vividly this beautiful lady who contacted me after watching my work and online presence for months. A resident psychiatrist with great potential, very bright, and extremely ambitious. This young lady was extremely beautiful, tall, and almost perfect, and on top of all that, she was smart. She was doing really well for herself, and she was engaged to a young entrepreneur guy that adored her. We felt great chemistry right from the start, and we decided to work together on what was unexpectedly her pain point.

She said, and I cite her: I know I am beautiful, everyone tells me that, and I can see it in the mirror or in the pictures, etc., but I cannot feel like I am beautiful, to enjoy my own beauty. As we discussed more and more, I found out she had a great fear for commitment even though she was engaged to be married and the traits of a nymphomaniac and a narcists. She was looking to sink into the arms of different partners on a side only to feel adored and to validate herself. She was kind, beautiful, ambitious, independent, well-mannered, sexy, and accomplished, yet she was all troubled.

What was her need? She had outside love, but she needed to feel important. She had this acute need for Significance, Importance, Relevance at a larger scale.

Another client of mine that I have known for quite a few years now and who is a very talented man put his entire focus on the need for safety, finance, and security while putting everything else on automatic survival mode.

He was a smart and capable man that worked 24 hours, and while he was unfit, unhealthy, single, and alone the biggest focus in his mind was how to make even more money.

Does my reader notice the mindset here, the need he priorities, the need he abandoned, and the aspects of his life that he completely ignored? I can confidently say that while we all know, including him, how important it is to stay healthy and fit and energized, he would constantly say to himself he was doing well because he was protecting the identity he built for himself.

One aspect he was doing ok was the business/work aspect; the rest of the departments was complete disarray: Love, health, and Entertainment.

His life was very predictable, a rigid lifestyle, and while you would expect a man of his intelligence to know better, he had a very rigid, unenjoyable, self-punished lifestyle.

He prioritizes in his mind only one need, the need for security, safety, and certainty of his immediate comfort.

All times are uncertain times, and while we know that, only when we really understand that we can ask ourselves the right questions that will direct to the empowering answers and prepare us for unpredictable experiences. So we don't wait for the future; we create by empowering ourselves in the process.

We asked the right questions, which allowed him to discover new ways, new opportunities in his business, to add new services and products in his business that allowed him to hire people to deliver; instead, he automatized a good part of his business which allowed him to start exercise, hired a fitness trainer, took swimming lessons and he is now in a loving relationship and about to get married.

However, the first step towards anywhere we want to reach in your life is to decide that you no longer want to stay where you are.

Think of your past as a tunnel that you embrace, you accept. At the same time, you realize you had to go through in a default mode and live these experiences for you to become the person that gets you where you're are today. The person you become today, to acknowledge the person you become today, and the strengths you develop will support your vision of becoming whoever you want to become.

The only evidence is what you become from looking back at your past and visioning the strengths you acquire from there to here.

Accept, embrace and move into the now and treat yourself as you are already the person you want to become.

Let go of the old and start creating the change that you need, the new you or the new situations. You start by creating new habits.

Nothing beats you worse than the way you beat yourself in your mind over and over again. Your weight is a direct reflection of your every single day eating and fitness habits. Your mood is a direct reflection of the cumulative repeated words you say to yourself. Your wealth reflects your major decisions or the lack of them. Stop beating yourself up and start acting consciously in creating the life you want for yourself.

It is the outcome you want, so the laser focus on your desired outcome will motivate your efforts.

YOUR NOTES

YOUR NOTES

About the Author

M any unexpected and unimagined things are happening in our lives, but changes are the most occurring nowadays and more than ever. The inevitable changes are the one that produces crisis, and we all know that crises are unwanted though they are the biggest motivators.

In this book written with love and humbleness, you will be reminded of everything you know and want to be reminded of. The book is a collection of thoughts, findings, and my personal perception about how we perceive life, what personal development really is and how to keep afloat when everything else sinks.

Awareness is power; however, understanding your personal why is more powerful than anything else in the whole wide world. Finding your why to your what and this is what this book is written in love, the joy of giving and tears of doubts it's all about.

We find more meaning in what we do when we really know why we are doing it!

What is your why to your what? If we think about our own thoughts, it's because we are the only living creature that can do that, and there is power in that.

Awareness is power; start your personal journey of success with a clear picture in mind. I can confidently say I had few pictures in the mind of what I wanted for as long as I can remember; those were to write a book, write a movie script, teach, be a psychologist, advocate, be a lawyer, and a famous person tv presenter. I never had a clear picture and so guess what? It took me a lifetime to acknowledge one.

A citizen of the world, born in Romania, I grew up surrounded by pain, rejection, insecurity, struggle, and scarcity. I was doomed to fail more than anyone I personally know, and I say this in absolute honesty, yet I am here today a living proof that we are what we think and want to be, no less, no more.

I lived and grew without the presence of a father; he would come once or twice a month completely wasted and ready to terrify my mom, and as my mom was working most days and nights to provide, then I was constantly lacking love, guidance, and attention. My mom had me to her own surprise and shock when she was 44, and by the time she was entitled to retire, she had a girl to raise that behaved and acted rebellious and boyishly on top of all that.

I spent three dreadful years in an orphanage for girls only, located in my town, where I learned injustice, aggression, humiliation, and hunger.

I was tiny, thin, dark hair, dark skin, and taller than the rest, while the standard features were blue, green, and hazel eyes with white pearly skin. I was never selected for anything other than to run chores, not for the gymnast's team or dancing or singing groups, and I felt I was naturally lacking in everything.

I have been bullied more than I have been said hello to, criticized, and constantly reminded that I am dark, thin, black, tall, or a gypsy.

I was used as a go and did or go and get in my own family, and see your place with this big nose, lips, feet, and hands. I suffered every day, yet I laughed and shared the joy with every occasion I could have. The failure of others made me feel like I failed myself, and I had natural-born wisdom to know better, especially for the people around me and myself.

All that was trivial as I couldn't make myself heard, and I couldn't change my condition, so you see, my lovely reader, I had to change myself despite my conditions and the circumstances.

I was born with an immense and tremendous need for love and affection, and while I was deprived of it, I continue to give it to the people around me that need it the most.
However, I was bullied at home and at school. I was verbally abused and beaten up for three years while in that school to the extent that would make any empathetic heart burst in pain and tears. Yet, in defense, I was continuously hungry, scared, ready to fight, and had this immense feeling of abandonment.

The constant lacking of food made us eat the apple fruit right after the flower season and before it had the chance to turn into a proper fruit. We were to eat anything that grew in trees, and even though my mom bought sweets and groceries twice a week. I never got the chance to eat because it was taken from me the minute I got into the dormitory.

Going back to when I was six: The first year in school, I was fortunate to have my first mentor, my first teacher in primary school, and I was only six years old. I never let her go, and I loved her dearly, of course after my mom, who was my entire universe of love and affection. I learned that education is crucially important in my teacher's house and that men are not necessarily drunks or aggressors of their wives.

My teacher Mrs. Caluianu needed me, and I needed her, and slowly the kids in my class respected me, and I was having a normal kind of life. But, I was craving for my mom's love, time, and attention, and she would give it to me every moment that she had while she was mostly at work, church, or helping other people in need.

Then when I was eleven years old, she got sick, and eventually, she needed to be hospitalized. After that, she really got worried about my progress and education, so she decided to place me in that school for orphans' girls as no one else was there to take me in.

I wouldn't bother you or my heart with vivid memories of my horrific times in that place, but I have missed my mom every single day and night though she visited me every chance she had. I suffered abandonment, aggression, abusiveness, hunger, and rejection.

I even ran away one evening from the "school", came home, and hid in the closet while waiting for my mom to come home. I planned to stay there until it was too late in the night for her to send me back, but I fell asleep while waiting, and by the dawn of the next day, I involuntarily stretched, so my mom was shocked to see me coming out of the closet.

One day, my mom visited me there at the orphanage to get me food, new clothes, sweets, and some pocket money, and as she left, she kissed me on my lips. As I turned to walk towards the after-school building, I licked my lips to avoid the wind of stealing her kiss. I was twelve years old. I loved, and I was loved all in fugitive moments.

Today I am here!

An intuitive transformational human with a versatile experience, a resourceful talented motivator that speaks from her heart and walks her talks. Nothing in this world will give me greater satisfaction than to know I bring some value into my readers' lives. I've been successfully coaching clients in their self-growth journey, but most importantly, I made a success of myself. So if you are feeling overwhelmed by life's demands, remember that nothing is permanent, and everything, in fact, happens for a reason; it could be a lesson we get or a lesson we give. Either way, it's a possibility to better ourselves. Our decisions determine the quality of our lives and are our actions that shape our path to success.

A professional coach possesses the ability to listen well and show things as they are, not worse than they are; however, a great coach has a firm grasp of reality with where you stand and helps you identify your goals, take accountability and deliver the best outcomes.

Powerful Affirmation: I have everything I need, right here in my heart, in my mind, in my spirit, and in my soul. It's in my blood, my body, and my heart that I am destined to heal and change the world into a loving place. Me, Monica Periade, I am a loving force of the universe with unlimited power to adjust the peace of the world.

Please replace my name and feel free to write yours. It's about you here, the Unstoppable You.

Quotes I love and quotes I wrote for you:

You can't take it with you, the Egyptians tried it, and all they got was robbed. Denzel Washington

The fear of rejection becomes your own rejection

Every woman is beautiful, and the more pain she hides, the more beauty she will transpire.

Expect nothing but be prepared.

It is you that can make things better for yourself as you are the only one that knows the cure you need.

If love can fade, so it's hate and pain.

Kind people are the best kind of people

The mind wants what the heart desires; feel it, place your inner palm on your heart and feel it.

Behind every smile, there is a genuine generosity that matters the most.

Chose kindness above all, chose love over ego.

In the midst of doubts, find the courage to be you. Simplify.

If you live to prove to others, you have not lived at all. -Coaching Lives & The Anatomy of Happiness.
Who you become in the middle of the chaos is who you are meant to become.

I am not the draft of art; I am the artist of my work.

People's lives are a direct reflection of their limitations.

Take a U-turn and cross on the opposite side of your limitations, it's not a U-turn but an I turn into something great.

There is nothing genius about being a spectator, be the leading actor of your own play. Be part of the spectacle and celebrate that.

Vanity's a perfect trap, so is magnifying it.

What is taken for granted will eventually be taken away

Take the risk or lose the chance.

You are, or you are not; there is nothing in between.

It will never be a perfect time or perfect way, so make it work right now

Life is not a popularity contest.

Find your way to your what, and you will know your how.

The heart is a muscle; train it in kindness.

A broken piece in a velvet box is still a broken piece; the work starts inside.

Be grateful to you, for you, about you.

Your success is to enjoy life, make it happen.

Other Books and Services by the Author

The sounds of unspoken words.

The end of the dawn.

Mentoring Program: The Science of Achievement.

Art of Fulfillment Coaching Lives:

http://www.monicaperiade.com/

Instagram: https://www.instagram.com/milleniumcoach/

Facebook: https://www.facebook.com/mileniumcoach

TikTok: www.tiktok.com/@milleniumcoach

Twitter: https://twitter.com/mperiade

LinkedIn: https://www.linkedin.com/in/monicaperiade/

Website: http://www.monicaperiade.com/

Podcast: https://anchor.fm/monica-periade

One More Thing Before You Go...

I f you enjoyed reading this book or found it useful, I'd be very grateful if you'd post a short review on Amazon.

Your support really does make a difference, and I read all the reviews personally, so I can get your feedback and make this book even better.

If you would like to leave a review, then all you need to do is click the review link on Amazon here:

If you would like to leave a review, then all you need to do is go to the review link on Amazon here: https://amzn.to/3dTscB4

Thanks again for your support!

Printed in Great Britain
by Amazon